NIKOLE KITTLING

Grace Made Me Do It

Copyright © 2022 by Nikole Kittling
Kavod Ministries Publishing

All rights reserved. Printed in the United States of America. No part of this book may be used or reproduced in any manner whatsoever without written permission except in the case of brief quotations embodied in critical articles or reviews.

Unless otherwise noted, all Scripture quotations are from the New King James Version®. Copyright © 1982 by Thomas Nelson. Used by permission. All rights reserved.

Scriptures marked NLT are taken from the HOLY BIBLE, NEW LIVING TRANSLATION, Copyright© 1996, 2004, 2007 by Tyndale House Foundation. Used by permission of Tyndale House Publishers, Inc., Carol Stream, Illinois 60188. All rights reserved. Used by permission.

ISBN for Paperback: 979-8-9871375-9-8

Printed in the United States of America

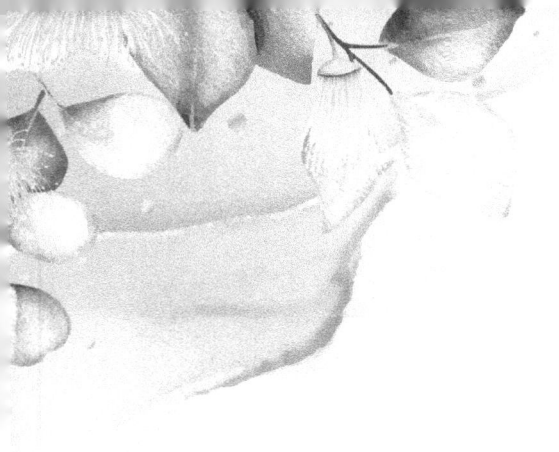

Dedicated to my daughters, *Alexis* and *Aleyah*.

You have seen me go through mountains high and valleys low… yet your love toward me was unwavering. You two inspire me and give me strength to keep going.

TABLE OF CONTENTS

Acknowledgments VII
Introduction IX

Chapter 1: Grace to Live 1
Chapter 2: Grace to Grow 15
Chapter 3: Grace to Fight 23
Chapter 4: Grace to Wait 29
Chapter 5: Grace to Stay 37
Chapter 6: Grace to Run 43
Chapter 7: Grace to Fast 51
Chapter 8: Grace to Love 59
Chapter 9: Grace for the Gift 65
Chapter 10: Grace to Win 73
Chapter 11: His Abounding Grace 79
Chapter 12: His Saving Grace 85

Prayer For Grace 91

ACKNOWLEDGMENTS

My gratitude goes to those who encouraged and inspired me to write this book. I thank those who have spoken prophetically into my life to reveal the plan of God. I am grateful to all of you.

Special thanks to my family, friends, and 3SC. I will never be able to express my gratitude for their support and all the extended phone calls. I am blessed to have them in my life.

I also want to thank all my church family and friends. I have been inspired and blessed by those who have poured abundantly into my life as prayer partners, confidants, and so much more.

I thank Jesus for it ALL!

INTRODUCTION

The clock starts ticking the moment we are born, and change begins whether we like it or not. People, places, and things will change on this journey called life, and along the way, we may fall... several times. At least, I did.

I used to believe that God was a good God as long as I was good. So I tried to live the "good" Christian life — whatever that meant. It was my perceived lifestyle. However, I found myself angry, frustrated, and far from being happy. I became spiritually drained and failed at my every attempt to please Him; it just did not seem to be working out for me, and I felt I did not have His grace or favor on my life. Nevertheless, I still wanted to try to live up to that ideal.

I remember having a long commute home in Atlanta traffic. All I wanted to do was fall on the floor when I got in, telling my children, "Mommy is going to time-out; may your angels watch over you," meaning that I was going into my bedroom closet — aka my prayer closet.

On one of these days, I went to my prayer closet to vent. Tired and fed up, I needed to have a little talk with Jesus and tell Him all about it. I remember saying out loud, "Look! I'm tired of trying to be this perfect Christian you want me to be. I am not that person. I make mistakes and will keep on making them. I can't do this."

After I rolled my neck and told God exactly how I felt, there was total, utter silence. Standing there, I stated, "Now, I have said all I have to say." Suddenly, I heard that still, small voice inside me say, "Thank you! Will the real Nikole please stand?"

Thus began my journey of grace.

Through study, I learned that the concept of "grace" referred to God freely extending Himself to us, translating to His favor and kindness reaching out to us because He is inclined to bless us — not because we are good, but because He is.

And although I have experienced both incredible and hurtful life-changing experiences, I discovered how this grace had played a significant role in my life, which is why in this book, I share an account of the acts of grace that flowed even during the times I was unaware.

Today, I can honestly say His favor and grace are upon me… and prayerfully, by the time you complete reading and working through the reflections that will follow, you will realize the same.

CHAPTER 1

Grace to Live

There was no ray of hope in sight. My heart quaked with fear. It was like being in a shootout, and the gunman had a 35mm revolver — locked and loaded. The enemy pulled open the cylinder and gave it a good spin. He pulled down the hammer and then pulled the trigger. Boom!

The first shot fired… Boom! He hit my body, and the doctor issued a diagnosis in 2008. I reached a point in my career where I felt ready to advance. I decided to return to college to obtain a second degree. I worked full-time by day and attended college at night. Somehow, I learned to manage work, family, and school. Things were progressing. Suddenly, I began to experience a series of random physical ailments. Initially, I noticed swelling in my ankles, feet, and hands. The doctor told me it was just edema and prescribed water pills. I figured I was overexerting myself and shrugged it off.

Then there was another occurrence. I woke up one morning and could not raise my right arm. I learned I had a torn rotator cuff. The doctor gave me cortisone shots, telling me to take a boatload of Aleve. The pain in my arm dissipated, but Aleve wreaked havoc in my stomach. So, back to the doctor I go. I complained of severe stomach pain. We tried everything, yet the stomach pain would not go away. We discovered that Aleve had eaten my stomach lining, compromising my gut health.

My eating habits had begun to change, and I no longer maintained a healthy diet. I noticed a decrease in my appetite and ate less often. Subsequently, weight loss occurred, and I dropped from a Size 12 to a Size 6 in a matter of weeks. My family and friends were concerned and frequently asked if I was okay. I did not know what was going on either, nor the reason for the drastic weight loss.

Finally, my primary doctor recommended a specialist and referred me to a Gastroenterologist. After a battery of tests, the results indicated an autoimmune disease called Crohn's. Immediately we started treatment in an effort to slow down the progression and enter into remission.

Of course, I was unable to work during the treatment and recovery stage. I grew weary and began to fear that I would lose my job. Luckily, I had a great manager. He was highly supportive and reassured me everything would be okay upon my return. After several months, the treatment was successful, and the disease entered remission. By God's grace, I recovered quickly and returned to work.

The second shot was fired… Boom! He hit my finances. A great recession hit the United States. We were facing an economic downturn, and everyone felt the stress of businesses closing and looming layoffs. But I was not concerned. Remember, my manager had assured me my job would be available when I returned. Well, it was not! The position I held became nonexistent. However, due to FMLA guidelines, the company made every effort to retain me. I was transferred to another department in hopes of retention . . . at least until all the economic uproar settled. But the rumors and reports of more layoffs continued to loom.

Nonetheless, all the rhetoric did not disturb me. I remember a coworker asked me if I was afraid. I told her nope! I walk by faith, and God will still provide for me no matter what. Besides, they gave me a new position, and I felt safe. Sure enough, a few months later, it happened. In 2009, I was laid off. As you can imagine, my livelihood was significantly impacted. We could not maintain our living expenses and eventually lost everything.

This shot slowed me down emotionally as well as financially. The million-dollar question everyone asked was, what do I do now? I did not have a clue as to how to reacquire everything I lost in an economic crisis. This shot stung and left a mark.

The third shot was fired… Boom! He hit my marriage. Surprisingly, I thought my marriage would be "till death do us part." When we first met, he just stared at me. I must admit it was weird and a bit uncomfortable. I wondered if he knew that was rude, so I asked him. You do know it is rude to stare, right? Then we both burst out into laughter. As we dated, we discovered we had a lot of things in common. I was previously married with kids. He was previously married with kids. Cool! We agreed on family matters, marital goals, and, most importantly, our Christian faith. My children grew fond of him and vice versa. Things were off to a great start!

He was active in ministry also and served as a Sunday School teacher at his church, which was different from mine. We had different styles of worship. He was more traditional, and I preferred contemporary. I am a little more active in my worship. I appreciate hymns from time to time, but I also enjoy praising the Living God I serve. The differences caused a little friction, but we moved past it and joined another ministry we both liked.

Finally, we were able to move on and focus more on blending our families. Besides, we have the same parental guidelines and expectations, so this would be a breeze. Boy, was I wrong! We did not see eye to eye on parenting after all. I was cussed out, disrespected, and ridiculed in my home without anyone intervening. I may be old school in parenting style, but if I ever fixed my mouth to curse an adult in my mom's presence, I probably would not be alive to tell the story.

The family unit was not blending but breaking. This caused turmoil in our marriage, and we hoped for reconciliation. Blended families can be challenging to interconnect; however, things can go smoothly when the parents stand strong in unity.

This incident made the boat rock, metaphorically speaking. From that point, things swiftly began to spin out of control. Everything I thought we had agreed upon in the beginning slowly unveiled true beliefs and value systems. Yes, we worked through many differences, from worship styles to parenting issues, but that was nothing compared to the real marital problems that rapidly appeared.

It seemed like everything I believed was false! I could no longer keep up with the lies, deception, and demonic attacks. I am known to be a fighter, but this one wore me down. My health was greatly affected by the stress and spiritual warfare endured in this marriage. And before he knew it, the boat tipped over, and I walked away. I did not have the spiritual stamina to stay in that marriage one moment longer.

This shot left quite a few bruises on me, but more sadly, our children also felt the impact. Here I go, picking up the pieces and starting all over again! However, grace was given to me. This hit slowed me down, but it did not stop me. I moved out.

The fourth shot sounded... Boom! The gunman hit me again, and I found no place to live. After the divorce, I felt smothered by the memories and the several failed attempts to reconcile. I needed to get away and have a change of scenery. Therefore, I moved to Florida in 2017.

I used to fantasize about living in Florida! My sister and I would talk about moving there all of the time. Near the coastline, it's known for its warm sub-tropical climate, amazing weather, and many beaches. Then one day, God gave me a prophetic dream. It revealed we would actually move to Florida, and my sister would move before me. Sure enough, several months later, she was offered a job in Tampa. By the way, she did not apply for this job. The job came to her. That is God's favor in action.

Shortly afterward, I headed to Florida to live with my sister. She already had one roommate and an extra room. When I moved in, we were all in agreement, and things took off quickly. I was blessed with a job right away. I was excited to be in the Sunshine State for my new beginning. A place I could put my toes in the sand and forget about the past. I was off to a great start. So, I thought.

Maybe two or three weeks after I moved, Hurricane Irma was heading to Florida. I guess she was a part of the welcoming committee. This was not what I expected, and I did not feel the love. I remember all the news stations broadcasting the event. Florida Governor asked all residents to evacuate. "Go get sandbags and board up your homes," he warned. I had no idea about what was happening or what to do. I was almost scared to death! We evacuated and went back to Georgia until all of that was over.

When I returned to work, the manager decided to terminate me; he said it was due to no-call/no-show. I was in disbelief. The entire world knew Hurricane Irma hit Florida. In addition, I had informed him of my evacuation plans. I guess Floridians have secret intel on how long it takes for the hurricane to move out and for employees to return to work; however, I did not get that memo. I was starting to feel the sunshine leave the Sunshine State. Where is the love, Florida?

Back to square one. I had to start job hunting again. But around that time, I noticed my health was beginning to fail, and I was hospitalized for several weeks. Upon discharge, I was instructed to follow a strict medicine regimen, and since the doctor wanted to ensure that my living arrangement was conducive to my healing and recovery, she asked about it. I assured her I was in a great environment and returned home to begin my healing journey, which would take several months.

Well, it was not there. After losing my job, the enemy came in like a flood, and Hurricane Irma had nothing on this one. I was minding my business trying to survive, and the roommate started having beef with me. She often made snide remarks to me with a sneer on her face. It quickly got ugly and nasty, but I was fighting to recover, so I let it roll off my back. Things escalated, and she became disrespectful and hostile towards my sister and me.

One day I was in the kitchen, and I overheard her yelling at my sister in rage. "Is she about to fight my sister?" I asked. Hurriedly, I walked to the hallway in an attempt to diffuse the situation. She started yelling at me. The next thing I noticed, she raised her hand to hit me. It was all over at that point. I grabbed her hand and snatched her up so fast she did know what hit her. I still had a little fight in me, lol. Nevertheless, she threatened to call the police on me, and I was told to get out! My name was not on the lease, so I had to leave. I had nowhere to go and knew no one in Florida. I grabbed a few of my things, put them in a hamper, and left. I became homeless. This shot wounded me and left me staggering.

Just when I thought the dust had settled, the fifth shot fired... Boom! To prevent the possibility of me rising again, the gunman became strategic with the two remaining bullets. He zeroed in on his target until my children were in the crosshair. The gun went off, and I took another hit in 2018. My daughters spread their wings and flew, which most parents would appreciate and be proud of. The problem was they flew away in different directions without looking back. The trajectory of their lives changed, and there even came a time when all communication was cut off.

I was devasted and tormented by the thoughts of the unknown. I literally did not understand what happened to our relationship or how it happened.

My soul cried out, and I felt crippled inside. I never imagined going a day without talking to them, much less weeks or even months. Amid battling previous shots by the gunman, I did not realize the relationship with my children would be attacked. I guess any open target would do for the enemy.

Studies show that life-changing events such as health diagnoses, marriage/divorce, college, etc., can cause a range of emotional responses in people — including everything from frustration and anger to anxiety and fear. With all things considered, they were dealing with their own life decisions. Normally, we talked things out and communicated. But this time was different. Soon, our relationship became estranged and appeared to be beyond repair. After this shot, I fell to the ground and tried to drag my wounded body to a safe place. Blood oozed out of me, and I lay lifeless with nothing left inside of me. This was it! I could not take another shot and survive.

The final shot went off… Boom! I flatlined. The bullet left a hole in me, and I became numb. I lost it all. My strength and the capacity to strive forward were gone. This time he shot to kill. My health took another downward turn. The worst ever. The doctors exhausted all treatment options; they did not know what else to do. I lay there, gasping for hope and strength. There were actual moments I thought I was going to die.

As thoughts raced through my mind, I said, "Am I at the point of no return?" It certainly felt like it. Have you heard the adage, *Pull yourself up by your bootstraps?* Well, what if you do not have bootstraps to pull? The enemy had taken it all from me.

According to Maslow's hierarchy of needs, we have five categories of needs: physiological, security, social, esteem, and self-actualization. When a lower need is met, the next need on the hierarchy can be achieved. The first need on the hierarchy is physiological. These are basic needs such as water, food, shelter, and clothing. Wow, physiologically, I was bankrupt! My basic needs were not met. I was homeless, helpless, and hopeless.

As stated, I was attacked on every end within a short span of time. Exasperated by the shots, I felt like giving up. Who wouldn't, after experiencing brutal back-to-back hits without any reprieve? The enemy wanted to take me out, and at a certain point, I was willing to go because I had nothing left in me to fight. I was done! But God's grace *(favor and kindness)* kept me, giving me the strength to push through one more time. God made all grace abound towards me. He grabbed me at the lowest point in my life, picked me up, and cleansed my wounds. And the restoration process began.

He sent angels to provide, protect, and care for me. I was the wounded man in the Samaritan parable discussed in Luke 10:30-37. God sent good Samaritans along the road where I lay half dead to care for me. They were a blessing and helped to restore my life.

I cannot count all the ways God used others to provide for me. He sent spiritual parents, church members, family, and friends. Everyone had a hand in it. When I did not have food to eat, I was fed. When I did not have a place to stay, I was sheltered. When I needed a hug or laugh, loved ones were there. When I looked around and thought there was no help in sight, God provided.

In the fight for life, perseverance is survival. In her poem, "Still I Rise," Maya Angelou writes, "You may trod me in the very dirt but still, like dust, I rise." It was by God's grace to live that I am still here. I heard Him clearly say, "Look up, child. I am your present help in times of trouble." When the enemy comes in like a flood to wipe you out, and you have no strength to go on, remember He will give you His strength to overcome and to live through it.

> "So let us come boldly to the throne of our gracious God. There we will receive his mercy, and we will find grace to help us when we need it most." —Hebrews 4:16 NLT

Reflections of Grace

We have an enemy that comes to kill, steal, and destroy us. But Jesus said He came that we may have life and that we may have it more abundantly (John 10:10). Are you in a health crisis? A financial turmoil? A relational challenge? You are not alone.

Take a moment to ask God for help. Then reflect on those times when you found grace to overcome life's battles.

GRACE TO LIVE

GRACE MADE ME DO IT

GRACE TO LIVE

CHAPTER 2

Grace to Grow

I started attending church at an early age. I learned fundamental principles of growth and development in the church. One of the basic principles was to read Scripture. It laid a foundation for me. When things got rough, I could always go to the Word to reset. He gave me the grace to grow in the knowledge of Christ.

In my first year of college, I got pregnant. My whole world was turned upside down, and I did not know what to do. I was angry and wanted to fight the father (just joking). I always had a lot of anger inside me, even as a child coming up. I fought all the time. I fought the neighborhood boys, school enemies, and even my sister's frenemies. And I was rather good at it. But when I got pregnant, I realized I could not fight my way through it. I needed to grow up.

I went to church one day, and there was a guest speaker. I cannot tell you what she said throughout her message. All I knew by the grace of God was that I needed deliverance, so after the service, I asked her to pray for me. I needed God to deliver me from anger which was really masked by hurt and pain.

Eventually, I calmed down and we got married. I became a young mother and a young wife simultaneously. I was completely clueless about life, marriage, and motherhood.

One of the guiding forces in my life was the Huxtables from the *Cosby Show*. They exemplified a two-parent home and marriage. I also read Dr. Spock's book about parenting. However, I quickly learned those references were not my reality. I was in a different world. What I was going through as a mother and wife were not on television or in a book.

I happen to be the youngest of eight siblings. You know how the story goes. The baby of the family can be prideful and tries to prove themselves; the youngest feels the need to be right all the time, and I am no different. You could not tell me anything, not a single thing! My mentality was to get on board with me or get left. But I needed help.

I experienced my first pain of motherhood when my oldest daughter could not keep milk on her stomach. She was only a few months old. After each feeding, she would spit up milk. It got worse, and she would vomit what seemed like air from her belly. It hurt me so badly to see my baby in that condition. I took her to the doctor, and he said she was having projectile vomiting.

He suggested I add baby cereal to her bottle and see if that would help. Well, I did, but it did not help. I went back to the doctor, and he told me to add more. I did, but it grew worse.

My mom witnessed and went through this experience with us. One day, she told me to stop putting cereal in her bottle. She believed it was the cereal causing her to vomit. I told her I was going to do what the doctor said. She said she had eight children, and she knew what she was talking about. I then said something mean and hurtful to my mother. I told her, "I am her mother, and he is the doctor." My mother was hurt. Still, she humbly agreed and walked away.

Guess what? The problem continued. Finally, the doctor became perplexed and said, "Okay, stop adding cereal to her bottle. Let's see how that works."

Sure enough, that worked, and the projectile vomiting ended. My mother had the solution all along, but I was proud. I did not want to receive what she told me. I observed her act of humility throughout this experience; she did not get angry or say, "I told you so." However, she taught me how to grow in grace. She showed grace towards me as a young mother and offered advice. When I rejected it, she simply surrendered to my request. At that moment, I grew up. I thought I had it all together. I thought I could navigate motherhood and marriage without any help. I was sadly mistaken and failing miserably.

> I wanted to escape me, so I hid in the Word.

I went back to my roots and the foundation that church had laid for me. That was to read the Bible and seek God in all things. My search began. One day I sat at the kitchen table with my head in my hand, staring at the Bible. I prayed and asked God to help me! "Give me the understanding of what I read in the Bible," I exclaimed. "I need your guidance. Show me how to live and be humble. I want to understand your will for my life."

For the first time, I began reading the Word with understanding. I could not believe it, but it clicked and made sense. I read like never before, especially during those obscure times in my life; it built my faith, trust, and confidence. Finally, I was on a journey of growth.

I began to attend church regularly and enjoyed reading my Bible. I hid in the Word because it was a place I found refuge. Some people enjoy reading self-help books, novels, or magazines. I found my interest in the Scriptures, and it drew me closer to His will for my life.

Subsequently, I learned how to pray, and change took place. I was growing in grace! I learned how to be nicer to my husband. Although, by the end of the week, I had to learn that particular lesson all over again. Nonetheless, change was starting to take place, and it was obvious.

> As life happens, grace to grow is happening too. Grow in Grace!

I have evidence to prove it. I have a sister-in-law that I love dearly. Let's call her "Wild Bill." We had a lot in common. She loves the Lord, reads the Bible, and is always ready for a fight. She would come out of the bushes! Be ready! She came to visit me, and we did what we normally do. We spent hours laughing and talking about life.

Suddenly, she stopped in the middle of our conversation and said in a serious voice, "Nicci, you have changed! If God can change you, then I know He can change anybody." Then we burst out laughing!

Life's lessons can cause us to grow and develop spiritually like muscles. It may not be apparent during the process, but the outcome will be greater. Yes, I had to go through some things to help me grow, but Jesus was there, guiding me through knowledge and understanding. It's good to know that as life happens, grace to grow is happening too.

> "But grow in the grace and knowledge of our Lord and Savior Jesus Christ. To Him be the glory both now and forever. Amen." —2 Peter 3:18

Reflections of Grace

In life, we will have many opportunities to grow; however, we must make the decision to take advantage of those opportunities as they present themselves to us.

Take a moment to reflect on what has gotten in the way of your personal and spiritual growth. Then, consider how you can choose to overcome those obstacles so that you can grow in His grace.

GRACE MADE ME DO IT

GRACE TO GROW

GRACE MADE ME DO IT

CHAPTER 3

Grace to fight

My eldest daughter and I had such an awesome relationship; we talked all the time about everything. I told my daughters they could talk to me about anything. Subsequently, my oldest daughter told me everything.

However, things changed when she moved away to college. She was busy being a college student. Eventually, the calls home began to decrease. I felt like I was losing one of my best friends. I was told when children go off to college, something strange happens — they stop calling home. I should expect the separation. Still, it was difficult.

After college, she moved further away to start a career. The chasm grew wider. I figured once she settled in, we would reconnect again. However, things sped up for her. She got married to a great guy and later had my first grandbaby, Armani Reign. Of course, I expected the dynamics of our relationship to change after marriage, but it seemed as if, in the twinkle of an eye, it all came crashing down! Our conversations became brut and crude. I was completely clueless about what had happened to our relationship. We went months without speaking. We had a few brief phone calls now and then. However, whatever I said seemed to upset her.

As time went by, there was no communication between us. My heart ached every day. I cried out to God and asked friends to pray with me. I knew this was an assault on our beautiful relationship, and I was determined to see restoration. I kept fighting by faith. I continued to trust God and made declarations. I prayed that she would forgive me for whatever I had done wrong, asking God to heal our relationship. By God's grace, I was persistent in my fight. I kept calling. I kept texting. I continued to send "I love you" text messages.

Honestly, I did not want to do it because I was hurting too. I felt rejected but decided to die to my flesh to see the power of God work in our lives. This is how I fight my battles. My mother taught me the importance of humility in a battle, so I swallowed my pride. I believe my daughter was also hurting; therefore, I kept sending her sweet and kind words via text messages.

During those moments, something was happening in the spiritual realm. Each time I sent a text message or prayed for her, it was like a hammer hitting a rock — blow after blow. I was fighting in the Spirit. I continued to strike that rock of bitterness with gentle, loving, and kind words. Finally, the rock was broken into pieces, and there was a breakthrough. As you have read, I am a fighter. But this time, I applied different techniques — I fought for our relationship in the spiritual realm through prayer.

After months of praying for our relationship, I went to visit her. She was pregnant at that time. I was so proud and happy. I was also nervous and prayed we would get along throughout my visit. My desire was to take her shopping and make sure they had everything they needed.

Well, surprise, surprise... she had a pleasant gift waiting for me! She had bought a self-care journal and placed it on my bed so I could see it the moment I arrived. It melted my heart, and began our journey of restoration.

Right before my flight back home, she opened up about her feelings of anger and pain. She needed to know she was loved and accepted by me. I was not aware that she had held this in, suffering silently for years. After she shared, I asked her to forgive me. There were a lot of things I did not do right as a young mother. Then, I asked if we could start over and rebuild. She agreed. Now, we talk every day, literally! God healed and restored our relationship.

Fight like God.

It was God's grace that kept me fighting through rejection. Fight like God by hitting the rock with the Word of the Lord until victory is won.

> "Is not My word like a fire?" says the LORD, "And like a hammer *that* breaks the rock in pieces?"
> —Jeremiah 23:29

Reflections of Grace

Have you ever been blindsided or disappointed in your desire for a healthy relationship with your spouse, parents, children, or other significant party? When you've given everything to those whom you love the most and things continue to fall apart, it can be devastating.

Take a moment to think of a time when, despite your best efforts, it was difficult to maintain a cherished relationship. Then, reflect on how you can embrace God's grace to fight beyond your own emotions.

GRACE MADE ME DO IT

CHAPTER 4

Grace to Wait

Are all college kids the same? I think so because it happened again. My youngest daughter graduated from high school at the tender age of sixteen — ready to move away from our small town.

When she was accepted at a university far from home, I told her that she had to attend a college within a two-hour drive, so that I would be able to reach her quickly if needed. But remember the youngest child syndrome? They think they have it all under control and will learn as they go. Actually, my daughter's favorite statement is *I will figure it out.*

Well, her father trumped me and she went off to college, and it was like déjà vu. "What's up with these college kids?" I wondered. Nevertheless, she was off to a good start and joined a great organization where she met new friends. Fortunately, she was able to adapt quickly to her unfamiliar environment.

On the other hand, I did not. The calls home became fewer until they eventually stopped. I felt like Job in the Bible. The thing I feared the most had come upon me... my baby had forgotten all about her mom.

My heart ached every day! It felt like years had gone by without hearing from her and my calls went unanswered. On some nights, I could not sleep thinking about her and what she was up to. I thought she probably was out having fun, but I needed to hear her voice to make sure she was okay. It is just the heart of a mother. After several weeks, I became worried and prepared to visit her.

Before my planned trip, I asked the Lord to let me know she was okay. Then I received a call from her. What a sigh of relief! God will answer prayers. I pleaded with her to call me every now and then to let me know she was okay. She assured me she was fine and to stop worrying. I canceled my trip and believed we were back on track.

On the contrary, I felt her pull away from me even more. Then the calls completely stopped. I could not figure it out and wondered why? Again, I prayed relentlessly, "Lord, restore our relationship." One thing I know for sure is that the enemy does not deploy new tricks. He uses the same ones over again; they are just packaged differently.

I wanted to do what I do best, fight! However, my fighting skills would not work in this situation either. I had to redirect my efforts. Some people cannot be forced into anything. The more you push them, the more they pull. The more I called, the less likely she would answer. On that account, it was time to engage a new strategy. In my quiet time, I received a new set of instructions. I was ordered to wait. I waited begrudgingly, yet I gained the strength to wait. I stopped worrying and patiently waited. According to Isaiah 40:31, But those who wait on the Lord shall renew their strength.

Several years ago, I attended a church in Villa Rica, GA. I still remember one of the sermons the pastor preached, titled "How to hug a porcupine." Oh, that would still preach today. What I learned was that porcupines go into defense mode once threatened; they will chatter their teeth and produce a chemical odor to ward off predators. If the threat continues, the porcupine will turn its back, raise its quills, and lash with its tail. You dare not come too close lest you get hurt. That was pretty much what my daughter was saying. "I am all grown up now, so back off!" However, it was so painful to sit and wait.

She once used a similar analogy to describe her personality. She said, "Momma, I'm like a little puppy. If you just hold out your hand, I'll eventually come to you." What a revelation! We had different analogies; where I saw a porcupine, she saw and became the puppy in the story. So, I took her advice and waited until she wanted to connect. At first, I did not know how to hold out my hand. I only knew how to hug. Eventually, it became painful to repeatedly hug a porcupine.

Sure, I was frustrated and wanted to give up. I felt rejected... again. However, God was teaching me another lesson about grace. It was the lesson of waiting — a difficult lesson to learn when you want immediate results. Grace made me do it, and I waited with my arms open. Then it happened! She came to me.

God did it again! He healed and restored our relationship, and I gained another victory. It was better than it had ever been.

One of my favorite memories is when she saw my sincere heart. One day, she walked into the living room while I was lying on the couch. She came over, lifted my head, and rested it on her lap. She then began to gently rub my head and said, "Momma, I wish people knew you as I know you."

> Keep holding your hands out with great expectation.

I cried a river as my heart was healed that very moment. I am often misunderstood, but she saw me. She realized I wanted to repair and fix what was broken by any means necessary. Although my methodology may differ, my heart is pure. I believe God gave me double for my trouble. She is married to a great man also, and I am blessed with two awesome sons.

If you are waiting for someone or something to change, keep holding out your hand in great expectation. Do not lose hope; the Lord will give you the grace you need to wait. He waited for us.

> "So the Lord must wait for you to come to him so he can show you his love and compassion. For the Lord is a faithful God. Blessed are those who wait for his help." —Isaiah 30:18 NLT

GRACE TO WAIT

Reflections of Grace

It is hard to wait when you are hungry! It's even more of a challenge when there is a long wait to get what you need. Take a moment to think about a time when you were hungry for a solution but there was a delay to receiving it. Then, reflect on how you can learn to have patience and gain the grace to wait.

GRACE MADE ME DO IT

GRACE TO WAIT

CHAPTER 5

Grace to Stay

Growing up, my mom made sure my sister and I went to church every Sunday. We participated in various church activities, including the youth choir, even though neither of us could sing very well. I remember the choir director called us to the piano to audition. He played a tune on the piano and asked us to repeat it after him. Well, we were obedient and did as we were instructed.

My sister sang first, and then it was my turn. We were so out of tune that he told us, "Y'all can't carry a tune in a bucket!" Nevertheless, he sent my sister to the alto section, and I went to the soprano section. That was one of the funniest things I experienced. We went to Vacation Bible School, youth retreats, and every program the church offered. Every time the door swung open, we were there! At some point, I got tired of going to church all the time and did not want to stay. Across the field was a recreation center. I often thought of ways to leave and go to the recreation center.

Little did I know that God was building a foundation. As kids, we did not understand why we were going to church. We thought it was only an opportunity for us to play with our friends and eat snacks. Boy, I still remember those cookies.

Nevertheless, something began to happen. Things change when you hang out in certain places or around certain people. You do not have to do anything; just show up. There was no action needed on our part for something to happen. All we knew was that our mother made sure we were in that environment. I guess she knew one day we would understand.

By the time I was a teenager, I had begun to take an interest in church service. I tried to follow along with the pastor's sermon and finally understood the message. The foundation was laid, and I began to build on it. How did it happen? I just hung out and dwelled in an environment where grace was present. I did not know it, see it, or feel it. But God was working out something in me.

I am reminded of the movie *Karate Kid*. In the movie, a teenage boy asks a karate instructor to teach him how to fight. The instructor agreed and told the young man to come every day at a certain time. The young man would show up every day faithfully. But every time he came, the instructor taught him to do odd jobs around his house. He was taught how to paint the fence and wax the car.

> There are people, places, or things that have the grace you need to grow.

The young man got so frustrated with the instructor. He told his instructor that instead of learning how to fight, he was just messing around at his house doing housework. He wanted to quit and leave! Little did he know the instructor was teaching him techniques and skills unbeknownst to him. As a result of those tedious household chores, he developed his skills and quickly became a champion.

I had the grace to stay in a church that did not seem to yield anything in my life. Boy, was I wrong! It yielded everything I needed to stay and develop tenacity. On the other hand, I do not want to be anywhere the grace of God is not. So, I encourage you to take a step back and ask yourself. Is this a place where I can grow if I stay? Can I operate in the fruit of the Spirit, which is love, joy, peace, longsuffering, kindness, goodness, faithfulness, gentleness, and self-control?

Stay... if grace is there — even if it seems like it is a waste of time. You never know what is growing underneath the surface. If He abides in that circumstance, He will give you the grace to stay.

> "So let it grow, for when your endurance is fully developed, you will be perfect and complete, needing nothing." — James 1:4 NLT

Reflections of Grace

There are people, places, or things that have the grace you need if you stay and develop. You may not be able to recognize it because it may be packaged as a job or relationship. Take a moment to reflect on how God's grace to stay was at work in your life and how your life was made better for it.

GRACE TO STAY

GRACE MADE ME DO IT

CHAPTER 6

Grace to Run

I first moved to Atlanta, GA, in 1997. It was time for a much-needed change. I chose to change the trajectory of my life in hopes of a better future. My family and I headed to Georgia with great expectancy. Everything started out great. We entered a good place in life, and things had finally settled down. At one point, I believed I would retire in Georgia and call it home. That is, until more life-changing events occurred.

Several years later, after the divorce and the girls moved away for college. I was standing on the precipice of a new life. "What should I do now?" I asked. All I wanted was to freely enjoy living in Atlanta without a husband and children. Georgia was on my mind as Gladys Knight sang. But after a wake-up call, I discovered that my soul was on God's mind!

I stood the chance of losing my soul and needed relief from all the drama. I wanted to anesthetize the pain of loneliness and fear. I made new friends and did new things. It was an attempt to kill the pain. Before I knew it, I was in a backsliding position and did not know how to get out.

My character changed, and I began to spiral out of control. I could feel myself slowly slipping away as the days went by. The more I felt it—the more I tried to ignore it. I was out of total alignment with the will of God for my life. The enemy can be so subtle and crafty. It always starts off as small movements before it escalates into an avalanche. I walked away from God and pursued my own desire. Providentially, Hosea 14:4 states, "I will heal their backsliding, I will love them freely, For My anger has turned away from him." Thank you, Lord, for turning your anger from me. His love never fails.

I am grateful for His mercy and longsuffering toward me. I knew I was out of His will when He gave me instructions to escape temptation. God will make a way to escape. He told me over and over again, "FLEE! Run from this situation." I had many opportunities to obey His voice, but pride and shame were in full effect. I did not flee. I thought I was in control of my life. I was sadly mistaken, lost, and confused. Yet, He still loved me.

There were so many times I wanted to walk away, but I could not. It was as if I was in a tidal wave. A force was thrusting me away and pulling me back in all at the same time! I felt like I had no control. What a frightening state to be in!

I tried to balance my desires with the will of God for my life. That, my friend, is called compromise, and it costs dearly. A friend told me a long time ago that the devil will take you to places you do not want to go and keep you there longer than you want to stay. And it was time for me to go!

One night, God gave me a vision I had never experienced before. In this vision, it was very dark, beyond midnight darkness, if that makes sense. I could feel the emotions in the dream. It was intense and cold. I heard in the still of this dark night, "your soul is required!"

I know the next part may question your theology, so hold on! I woke up crying and trembling. I knew this was a real message and not just another dream. The message was I was going to hell if I did not turn from my ways and back into His will. Yes, me — a person who accepted Christ and loved God. Some people believe that once saved, always saved. I don't know about that but allow me to tell you what I do know. I know that the Lord said to me that I was going to hell! That came directly from the Father. On top of that, you know the devil will never tell you that you are going to hell.

He also showed me how my children's lives would be affected as a result of my sin and disobedience. That vision pierced my heart and soul. I was done. I had to bust a move and flee because my soul depended on it.

Many Christians do not believe they can go to hell; however, the Bible states that the very elect will be deceived. Men came to Jesus and said, "I cast out demons in your name." Jesus said, "I know you not!" (Matthew 7:23 NLT)

Despite my rebellious ways and disregard for His commands, He was merciful and gracious to me. He gave me a second chance, and I ran! I literally ran out of Georgia.

If you are out of the will of God, ask Him to give you the grace to escape that situation. Anyone or anything that causes you to be out of alignment with the will of God for your life, run from it. He will give you the grace to do it. He instructs us to work out our own salvation with fear and trembling. In the next chapter, I will share His plan that restored my soul.

> "Therefore, my beloved, as you have always obeyed, not as in my presence only, but now much more in my absence, work out your own salvation with fear and trembling." — Philippians 2:12

Reflections of Grace

Although there are times when God gives us grace to fight and to stay, there are also times when He will clearly tell us to leave.

Take a moment to reflect on a time when you knew that He was directing you to remove yourself from a situation, yet you didn't heed His voice. Then consider how His grace kept you safe, giving you a second chance to align with His plan for your life.

....

....

....

GRACE TO RUN

GRACE MADE ME DO IT

GRACE TO RUN

CHAPTER 7

Grace to fast

My desire had always been to live a life of consecration through fasting and praying. I usually hit and miss it from time to time, but I wanted consistency because I would start the day off proclaiming a fast, yet by noon, I was eating a burger. I was disappointed in my lack of discipline. Fasting requires more than just a desire to be successful. I got angry most of the time because I felt like God was not answering my prayers when I fasted. Of course, that shorted-circuited my time of fasting as well. Then I began to learn about the power of fasting.

As I mentioned in the previous chapter, my health began to fail as soon as I moved out of Georgia. My body rejected food and I could not eat for days or weeks at a time. I guess you can say my body was being conditioned to fast, unbeknownst to me. I just needed to add prayer and call it a fast.

When I moved to Florida, it took quite some time to get back to normal. I regained my health and strength to return to work. I moved into a new place, and things were starting to look good. It seemed like I was back in alignment with God.

Then, I started having reoccurring dreams about Jesus calling me, literally. In one particular dream, I was asleep in bed. My best friend was alongside me. She slept on one side, and I was on another. In the dream, I heard a phone ring. Then, a person handed me the phone. I saw the name "Jesus" on the phone screen. Nowadays, most cell phones show you who is calling. On some phones, green and red dots appear, giving you the option to answer or reject a call. I grabbed the phone, then politely passed it to my best friend.

She answered and gave the phone right back to me. "They want to talk to you," she said. I did not want to take the call. Then, I woke up. I spent days trying to understand that dream and others like that one. It frustrated me. I asked for revelation and understanding, but I did not receive it. Until one day after church, the pastor called out to me. I walked over to him, and he asked how I was doing. I gave my usual response, "I am good." He stared at me for a moment. Then he began ministering to me and released a prophetic word. He said, "I see you in a corridor like a hallway, and the walls are beginning to close in. The walls are getting narrow as you walk, and it is dark at the end of it." Then, he told me to pray and really seek God.

Well, that did it for me! I was angry and grieved at the same time. I could not understand the message and needed revelation asap. I began to experience fear and anxiety. I asked, "God, what are you trying to tell me? I keep having these dreams of being called. I don't know what I am being called to or how to answer the call. If I don't answer, am I going to hell?" In exasperation, I sought and cried out for answers, and the only way was through fasting and praying.

Remember, the extent of my fasting meant skipping a meal or two. Regardless, I proclaimed a fast due to my desperation. I went into my prayer closet and cried out before the Lord. In prayer, I asked what I was being called to do. I prayed for an answer right away because I was in agony. I did not have a clue, but I did not want to miss it.

Later, I received instruction to fast for ten days by the Spirit of the Lord. Yikes, ten days! I was so hungry for the salvation of my soul that I did not second guess it. I committed to the fast. Immediately, I heard in my spirit, "solemn fast." That was the first time I heard that term and didn't know what it meant. So, I looked up the word *solemn* in the dictionary. It means "deep sincerity, being very serious and formal." In other words, this fast was no joke.

I knew it was serious, and my life/soul depended on it. For ten days, I was before the face of the Lord in prayer. I cried out sincerely in repentance with godly sorrow for my sins. I was so hurt and ashamed for turning my back on God. I felt like sin was being stripped away from me as I prayed. I did not tell my family about the fast because they would freak out. They had seen me suffer from Crohn's and would not understand why I was choosing not to eat. They did not understand the power of fasting… yet. They believed if I ate, I would get healthy. But I was more sin-sick than physically ill.

At a point in my fast, they noticed that I was not eating and asked if I was fasting. Of course, I did not respond. "You can't afford to fast because you are only skin and bones," they said.

> Fasting is not about getting... It's about GIVING.

They thought I needed to feed my flesh, but actually, my spirit needed to be fed. So, I prayed and asked the Lord to make a covenant with me that I do not lose weight while fasting. Well, He honored the request and faithfully held up His part of the deal, sustaining me as I fasted.

During the fast, Jesus began to minister to me as to why He died on the cross. I was reminded that the wage of sin is death according to Romans 6:23. It was His death that paid for my sins so I could have eternal life. I had taken that for granted for a moment in my life. However, I was desperate to be in right-standing with the Lord. Then He took me through a three-step process:

- First, I had to repent and open up the communication channel with God. Isaiah 1:15 shows that God will not hear your prayers until you repent.

- Secondly, I gained knowledge about the purpose and power of the Blood of Jesus. Sin must be atoned for through the blood. For it is the blood that makes atonement for the soul, according to Leviticus 17:11b. Jesus' blood was shed for the remission of my sins.

- Lastly, I needed to understand His love for me. This is real love—not that we loved God, but that He loved

GRACE TO FAST

us and sent His Son as a sacrifice to take away our sins. Jesus said, "There is no greater love than to lay down one's life for one's friend" (John 15:13 NLT).

By the end of the fast, my love and reverence for Jesus returned. My soul was restored, and I did not remain the same. According to 2 Corinthians 5:17, "Therefore, if anyone is in Christ, he is a new creation; old things have passed away; behold all things have become new."

Although I call that a successful fast, I am still growing and learning. One of the most powerful lessons the Holy Spirit taught me about fasting is that it is a transaction; I call it a fasting transaction. A spiritual transaction takes place when you fast. The Lord gently taught me a key principle: Fasting is not about *getting*; it's about *giving*. It is not about receiving something from me but about giving yourself to me. Give me your time, attention, and heart. In return, I will give you mine.

Finally, I understood the transaction that takes place when I fast. As a result, I have developed a lifestyle of fasting and praying. The Bible passage in Matthew 6:16-18 gives instructions on fasting. Therefore, when you fast or desire to fast, trust that God will give you the grace and strength to do it. It is already built inside of you; just make the transaction.

"For I can do everything through Christ, who gives me strength."—Philippians 4:13 NLT

Fasting is a spiritual transaction that produces a natural manifestation. Take a moment to ask God what, when, and how He wants you to take up a solemn fast. Then, reflect on how His grace to fast has been (or can be) evident in your life.

GRACE TO FAST

GRACE MADE ME DO IT

CHAPTER 8

Grace to Love

The love of Christ transcends all cultures and boundaries. I know this to be true, and it can happen at any moment. Do not miss the chance to receive and exhibit Christ's love. I had the opportunity to demonstrate His gracious love as I walked through the park one day.

Several years ago, I would visit a nearby park to enjoy the fresh air and scenery. Then I decided to come daily for a morning walk, noticing a lady who would arrive at the same time I did. One day we locked eyes, and I greeted her with a smile. Our conversation first began with small talk, but as time went on, the tone of the conversation changed; it was like the beginning stages of a friendship. We shared a little more about our family and occupation — her husband was completing his medical residency at a local hospital — and later, I inquired about her origin. As we often say in the south, "Where are you from?"

She disclosed that she was a Muslim from a Middle Eastern

country. Although she wore a scarf every morning, I did not identify her as Muslim. I identified her as my walking partner. It is not unusual for women to wear scarves in the morning. Furthermore, it did not matter to me.

Every day, we shared more about our personal lives. We began to look forward to meeting each other in the mornings. One day, she shared that terrorism was quite common in her country. It was under constant attack by Islamic extremists. They were in her hometown, often looking for recruits. Anyone who refused to join forces with them would be executed.

I shared that I had heard about the atrocities on the news. She told me that an extremist came to her parents' home and recruited her nephew. He became an extremist against his will. Her family was devasted. They lived in constant fear because they did not share the same faith as Islamic extremism.

While she spoke, her countenance changed, and we slowed down our pace; my heart became heavy and saddened as well. I did what was in my heart, showing love and compassion. I told her I was so sorry to hear that, and then I asked if it was okay for me to pray for her family and their protection.

With tears in her eyes, she whispered, "Thank you." At that moment, she discovered I was a Christian. This was awkward for her because it is not common for Christians to pray for Muslims. "You are different," she said. I simply smiled as we continued our walk. Then she proceeded to tell me about the horror of living next door to a Christian.

Upon moving to Georgia, they found a lovely home in the neighborhood. They were ecstatic to move into their new home and start their lives. Life was going well for them until their neighbor discovered they were Muslims. The neighbor harassed her every time she pulled up in her driveway. Sometimes, the neighbor would wait outside for them to come home to throw racial slurs at them. One evening after dinner, they arrived home. As they were walking to the door, the neighbor yelled and said, "I am a Christian, and we do not believe in your God. Just go back to your country to serve your God."

Let love live in you.

I was heartbroken. I could feel her pain of being constantly harassed. She said that it occurred often. Finally, she had enough! She spoke out and said to her neighbor, "Isn't your religion supposed to be about love? You claim to be a Christian, yet you hate my family. How can you be a follower of Christ, the Son of Love, but hate your neighbors?" I was stunned. She was right! Is this an appropriate way to represent Jesus? Is this how we portray the Spirit of Christ living within us to the world? Our walk should line up with our talk to represent Christ accurately. Let us pause and think about that for a moment.

In Matthew 22:39, Jesus commands us to love our neighbors as ourselves. My Muslim friend knew more about the love of Jesus than her self-proclaimed Christian neighbor. We ought to always walk in love and exemplify the love of the Father. Allow the love of Christ to flow through you always and live in you. You have the grace to love as Christ.

> "No one has ever seen God. But if we love each other, God lives in us, and his love is brought to full expression in us."
> —1 John 4:12 NLT

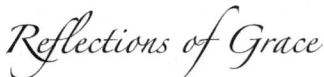

The Scriptures tell us that others will know we are Christians by the love we demonstrate to one another (John 13:35). So, have you had the opportunity to love someone who seemed unlovable or someone who is not like you?

Take a moment to reflect on how God's grace has helped you be an expression of His love.

GRACE MADE ME DO IT

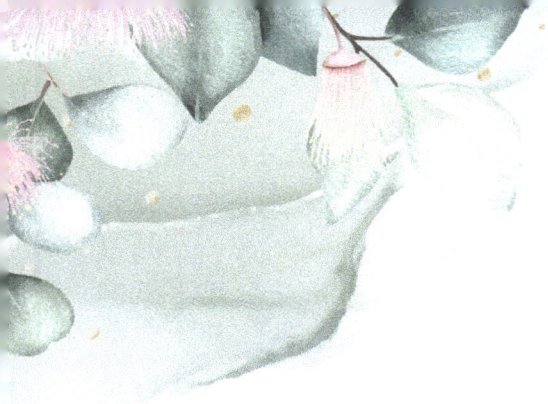

CHAPTER 9

Grace for the Gift

Over twenty years ago, I discovered I was a dreamer. I dreamed often and remembered waking up perplexed on most mornings. Most times, I did not have a clue what they were about. Other times, I was given revelation immediately.

Nonetheless, it became overwhelming, and I asked God to stop giving me dreams. Some dreams seemed so real that I questioned if they had meaning ... perhaps foretelling of something that would take place. Again, I lacked the understanding and purpose of the gift of dreams and interpretation; therefore, I prayed for the dreams to end.

Well, He answered my prayers, and they stopped. At first, I enjoyed the peaceful nights of sleep. Then, I started feeling disconnected from the Heavenly Father, like something was missing. I realized that dreaming was a form of communication that we shared, and I wanted it back. I felt awful and repented for my actions. I began to yearn for His presence and to dream again. For many years, nothing happened. As time went on, I began to dream again. I was extremely grateful; they served as a guide to prayer, revealing things for preparation or warning. I was able to understand certain situations in my life. Thankfully, the Lord was merciful and slowly restored them.

The Word of the Lord states that God's gifts and His call can never be withdrawn (Matthew 7:23). Spiritual gifts are given to believers who accept Jesus Christ and receive the Holy Spirit. Then the believer receives certain gifts from God to do the work of God in the body of Christ. That means spiritual gifts are purposeful. He does not regret giving a believer a spiritual gift, and He will not take back the gift. However, He may honor your request to remove it as He did for me.

Still today, I use that experience as a testimony. Whenever someone tells me they have dreams without understanding, I immediately tell them to pray for revelation and not take it for granted. God will give you understanding or send someone to interpret for you. Daniel and Joseph in the Bible also had the gift of interpreting dreams for others. He will not leave us without wisdom and understanding as we seek it.

> Embrace your gift.

Along with dreams and interpretations, I have been graced with the gift of discernment of spirits. This gift discerns between the Holy Spirit and evil spirits, especially when demonic activity is present. This gift is often used in spiritual warfare. I guess that is why I was a fighter by nature, so I could go to war in the spiritual realm. Consequently, I have earned my stripes to be a warrior.

I better understood this gift as I matured. However, it became clearer after an incident at church I attended in Atlanta. Every Sunday, there was a particular lady who stood at the front of the church during the altar call. Each time I saw her, I got a sense that something was not right and began to feel vexed in my spirit. I wondered if the pastor or others saw what I saw or felt what I felt. It was unsettling.

One day after service, my sister and I stood in the foyer to chat. Along came this same lady, approaching my sister to speak to her. I immediately shouted, "She's a witch! Don't talk to her." I then pulled my sister away, and she walked off. I was shocked at my outburst. That had never happened before; however, I knew it was divine. I knew by the Spirit that she was a witch. Nothing externally could identify her as such. She did not wear a black hat or ride a broom. It was the Holy Spirit that revealed it to me.

I think at that moment, I knew I had a spiritual gift. It is a gift freely given along with grace. This gift can be used to alert you of the presence of evil and darkness. As soon as I discern the works of darkness around me, I actively engage in spiritual warfare. I take authority over it and take it down in the spiritual realm because we are not fighting against flesh and blood, according to Ephesians 6:12.

On the other hand, not every experience has been evil or demonic. I have met people with the Spirit of Christ, and it was amazing. My sister was invited to have dinner with a friend. I came along as her plus one. I had never met her friend but heard good things about her. When I came into her presence, I wept. Tears began to stream down my face, and I felt the presence of the Holy Spirit. I thought, this lady must think I am bananas! I was compelled to share that I felt God's presence, and it was overwhelming. She said, "It is okay. I have been praying for you." Wow! I was speechless. Now I have learned to operate in grace when the gift of discernment is active. I no longer have outbursts when I recognize a demonic presence or weep profusely when I feel His Spirit.

God is all-powerful and the creator of all things, good and evil. Therefore, we should not be afraid of evil and wickedness because He has not given us the spirit of fear but of power. Likewise, He has given us His power which is the Holy Spirit, to discern His goodness as I did with my sister's friend.

God gives us the grace to handle the gifts He has bestowed upon us. Seek Him to grow and develop the gift He has given you and embrace your gift.

> "In his grace, God has given us different gifts for doing certain things well." —Romans 12:6a NLT

Reflections of Grace

Spiritual gifts are given to believers to edify, encourage, and comfort the body of Christ. They are recorded in 1 Corinthians 12. Take a moment to reflect on your spiritual gift(s) or how the spiritual gift of another has impacted you.

GRACE FOR THE GIFT

GRACE MADE ME DO IT

GRACE FOR THE GIFT

CHAPTER 10

Grace to Win

I am still writing this chapter of my life. Like King David in the Bible, my victories are too numerous to count. Although the battles he won are chronicled in 2 Samuel 8, I cannot list all my victories. I won battles that I did not fight. Yes, the Lord fights for us, and we get the victory. The Word of the Lord tells us in Exodus 14:14 that the Lord fights for you! So be still!

One of the most difficult things to do during a battle is to be still. When our back is against the wall, and we face a seemingly impossible situation, we have the urge to fight. Winning is not just about fighting. It's about trusting God to deliver you out of the storms of life and following His instructions to succeed. God will give you the right strategies to win.

The Lord gave me grace to follow His rules and orders. There are rules of engagement in war, which means I cannot use the weapon of my choice. I had to follow the God-given rules. Furthermore, every set of rules may not apply to every battle. There are operation-specific rules of engagement. You cannot apply the same tactics for every fight. So, it is in your best interest to follow the rules to win. If you fail to abide by the rules of engagement, you are subject to dire consequences.

I did not want to lose the battle with my girls; therefore, I obeyed the commands. The first order was to fight silently in prayer. Prayer is a weapon. Secondly, exhibit love amidst pain. Lastly, be still and wait. I did as I was instructed. Then, I trusted God to circumvent the plans of the enemy that wanted to kill, steal, and destroy our relationship. As a result, I got the victory and won the battle!

> Prayer is a weapon.

Remember, every battle is not the same. There were times I had to fight in battle. I fought most of my life, physically and spiritually. I felt like Oprah Winfrey in the movie *The Color Purple*... all my life, I had to fight! And I am still fighting, but I am not alone on the battlefield. I have all of heaven backing me up! The Lord of Host sends angels to fight for us. In addition, Jesus intercedes for us while the Holy Spirit is downloading intel. This is the mighty army; we are a part of the army of the Lord.

When facing a battle, be sure you consult with the Heavenly Commander-in-Chief for orders. In 1 Samuel 30:8, David asked the Lord if he should go chase down the enemy who stole everything from him. The Lord answered and told him yes, go fight! God wants you to win! He will send all of Heaven's Army for backup. Most importantly, with Christ, we have victory.

Check out a few of my victories:

Battle of Breaking Generational Curses – Won
Battle of Restored Relationships – Won
Battle of Peace of Mind – Won
Battle of Spirit of Rejection – Won
Battle of Freedom in Christ – Won
Battle of Healing/Health – Winning

There are more things I am winning in life. I have perfect faith that I will recover it all, just as David did. Let God's grace abide in you, and you will win.

> "So David inquired of the Lord, saying, 'Shall I pursue this troop? Shall I overtake them? And He answered him, "Pursue, for you shall surely overtake them and without fail recover all." —1 Samuel 30:8

Reflections of Grace

How do you fight your battles? Do you attempt to win in your own strength, or do you trust God's promise that you will be "More than a conqueror" (Romans 8:37)?

Take a moment to reflect on the battles He has won for you and the victories you have received through His grace to win.

GRACE MADE ME DO IT

GRACE TO WIN

GRACE MADE ME DO IT

CHAPTER 11

His Abounding Grace

Reflecting on all the things I have been through and overcame, I realized that I could have lost my mind amidst losing everything else. Yet, God kept me. I do not understand it all, but I am still here. I know others have endured far more trials and tribulations than I have. And I stand amazed with them. I often wonder how I made it through. I received grace to endure and overcome every attack and downfall. It was nothing but grace. Here is what I would say if I had to summarize it in a single verse (2 Corinthians 9:8):

> "And God is able to make all grace abound toward you, that you, always having all sufficiency in all things, may have an abundance for every good work."

God wants to bless us. He wants the nature of His personality to be evident in our lives. He is the author and giver of all benefits. Most large organizations offer benefits as a total reward program. But He offers the ultimate total reward package that includes eternity. It is hard to imagine, but we have obtained these benefits through Christ.

T.D. Jakes authored a book titled *Can you stand to be blessed?* I think that is a good question to ask. His blessings can overwhelm you ... in a good way. May the blessings of the Lord overtake you so you can richly enjoy His grace. Grace is power brought to us by Jesus Christ. Through Him, God extended His favor and grace to us. We did nothing to merit or deserve it.

Because of Jesus, we have grace. Grace to do all things for every good work. For years, I was in bondage because I did not understand how grace worked. I believed that God was standing at the door of heaven, looking down on me with a big tablet and pen, ready to check off all my wrongs.

> "Grace is the enabling of God not to sin; grace is power, not just pardon."
> -John Piper

I had the mindset of an unloved sinner. I often felt discouraged because I missed opportunities to be sinless. There was an imaginary Christian checklist in my head. Unfortunately, I believed I would never receive everything God had for me. Then I read Romans 11:6 NLT, "And since it is through God's kindness, then it is not by their good works. For, in that case, God's grace would not be what it really is — free and undeserved."

Wow! You mean to tell me that I cannot earn God's grace? No, it is extended to us because He is good. His grace is free to all and undeserved.

He is a gracious and giving Father. Receive His limitless grace for your life, and do not forget to tell others about this free gift.

> "But my life is worth nothing to me unless I use it for finishing the work assigned me by the Lord Jesus—the work of telling others the Good News about the wonderful grace of God." —Acts 20:24 NLT

Reflections of Grace

Have you received His free and undeserved grace? Take a moment to reflect on how His abounding grace is evident in your life and how you can extend that grace to others.

GRACE MADE ME DO IT

HIS ABOUNDING GRACE

CHAPTER 12

His Saving Grace

Do you remember when I stood in my closet and told Jesus, "I quit! I cannot be that perfect Christian you want me to be!" That was all He needed to perfect His work inside of me. He does not ask us to be perfect. He only asks us to come unto Him, and He will make us whole. We can take off the burden of trying to be perfect and end the madness of a religious checklist.

Jesus is love, pure love. No greater love than this, for a man to lay down his life for you and me. He said, "Come to me all ye that are heavily laden, and I will give you rest." Are you tired of the weight of life? Let the grace of God flow in your life. I do not know about you, but I wanted to rest from the battles of life. He just wants you to come, and He will do the work in you through the power of His Holy Spirit.

When my children call me, we talk about each other's day. There have been many conversations of how someone did something unfair and they disagreed with their actions. I often respond and say, "Give people room to grow." Let us show the same kind of grace we have received through Christ. Love people through it. Whether it is someone on your job, family member, or spouse, extend grace.

Our Father patiently waited for us to learn, develop, and grow. He sees the greatness inside of us despite our actions. We share similarities of a diamond in the rough and a pearl in an oyster. You may have been hidden or tossed like a raging sea but hold on until the end. His grace will find you and allow you to come through life's circumstances, shining bright like a diamond. Allow His grace to work in you and through you. Be the polish to shine someone else in their time of darkness. Encourage them and let them know they can overcome loss, pain, or illness.

> Give people room to grow.

With Christ Jesus, no matter how indisposed the situation is, there is a God that has grace for it.

As mentioned earlier, there is unlimited grace. There is amazing grace, sanctifying grace, and the gift of grace which is the Holy Spirit. But the most important of them all is Saving Grace which is the redeeming grace of God. His name is Jesus. The Scripture tells us in Titus 3:3-7 NLT:

> Once we, too, were foolish and disobedient. We were misled and became slaves to many lusts and pleasures. Our lives were full of evil and envy, and we hated each other. But when God our Savior revealed his kindness and love, he saved us, not because of the righteous things

we had done, but because of his mercy. He washed away our sins, giving us a new birth and new life through the Holy Spirit. He generously poured out His Spirit upon us through Jesus Christ our Savior. Because of His grace he made us right in his sight and gave us confidence that we will inherit eternal life.

We have been regenerated, renewed, and saved by His grace. Whatever you believe is impossible to do, ask our Father for the grace to do it. Better yet, receive the fullness of His grace which is Christ Jesus.

Grace made me do things I did not want to do. It made me do things I did not think I could achieve. But through Christ Jesus, our Savior, I won battles, and so can you!

> "God saved you by his grace when you believed. And you can't take credit for this; it is a gift from God."
> —Ephesians 2:8 NLT

Reflections of Grace

The grace of God has the power to effect change in our hearts and lives. It is not something that He owes us, but a gift that He lovingly gives us. Without it, we would be lost.

In this final reflection, take a moment to consider how His saving grace has affected change in who you were and helping you become a better version of who you were created to be.

GRACE MADE ME DO IT

HIS SAVING GRACE

GRACE MADE ME DO IT

PRAYER FOR GRACE

Gracious God, You have chosen me to be in a relationship with You. Through Jesus, You have extended amazing grace to me. By grace, I have been saved. Help me to understand Your grace abounds towards me to do your will.

Father, show me more of your grace at work in my life. Allow it to manifest even more this day so that I can extend grace to others. Your grace is sufficient.

Thank You, O my Father, for your Amazing Grace.

Amen.

www.ingramcontent.com/pod-product-compliance
Lightning Source LLC
Chambersburg PA
CBHW070949180426
43194CB00041B/1945